VERY MODERN
MANTRAS

DAILY AFFIRMATIONS
FOR DAILY AGGRAVATIONS

DAN ZEVIN

RUNNING PRESS
PHILADELPHIA

Running Press
Hachette Book Group
1290 Avenue of the Americas, New York, NY 10104
www.runningpress.com
@Running_Press

Printed in China.

First Edition: October 2019

Published by Running Press, an imprint of Perseus
Books, LLC, a subsidiary of Hachette Book Group, Inc.
The Running Press name and logo is a trademark of
the Hachette Book Group.

The Hachette Speakers Bureau provides a wide
range of authors for speaking events. To find out
more, go to www.hachettespeakersbureau.com or
call (866) 376-6591.

The publisher is not responsible for websites (or
their content) that are not owned by the publisher.

Additional copyright/credits on pages 166–167.

Library of Congress Control Number: 2019937465

ISBNs: 978-0-7624-6761-7 (hardcover),
978-0-7624-6759-4 (ebook)

1010

10 9 8 7 6 5 4 3 2 1

CONTENTS

CHANT, DON'T RANT.

Finding inner peace is extremely stressful. You try to visualize rainbows and waterfalls, but quickly start visualizing deadlines, appointments, and that weird rattling noise your car has been making when you put it in reverse. You do your best to focus on your breath, but wind up focusing on your broken phone, and on the hour you're about to lose live-chatting with a customer service representative who won't know how to fix it, and on the endless array of all the other daily aggravations you need to be focusing on instead of focusing on your breath. Sure, you can lock yourself in a darkened room and chant a katrillion *Oms*. But how about a mantra for waiting in line at Starbucks while the lady in front of you spends twenty minutes customizing her foam-free latte? Or a mantra for reckless sidewalk texters? Or a mantra for surviving a mind-numbing staff meeting? These are the daily aggravations that drive even the most mindful among us out of our minds. These are the moments we need some very modern mantras.

The sacred text you hold before you contains aggravation-specific, microtargeted meditations for today's world. Each begins with a rainbow-free visualization ripped from real life, and ends with a very modern mantra to chant over and over whenever you're about to lose your ~~shit~~ serenity. By making this book the center of your mindfulness practice, you will achieve instant inner peace. And if that doesn't pan out, I hope you'll get something we can all use on our daily slog toward #tranquility: a laugh.

Namaste,
Dan

MANTRA FOR STARBUCKS

Close your eyes and envision an infinite
line of humanity,
stretching miles and miles and miles.
Now, envision this line is at Starbucks.
At the front, notice a young woman in Uggs,
explaining how she would like her latte prepared.
Tune in to *her* needs.
She wants it one-quarter caffeinated, half-soy,
and no nutmeg . . .
Because she does not like nutmeg . . .
And what can they recommend to *replace*
the nutmeg?

As you realize you're going to be late for
your morning meeting,
visualize taking her aside . . .
And explaining to her that, despite everything
she has ever been told by her mommy . . .
The world does not *really* revolve around her.
Become keenly aware of your fists, clenching
tighter and tighter and tighter.
On the count of three, release them.
One . . . two . . . three.
Together we chant Modern Mantra #1 . . .

"I WILL NOT
LOSE MY SHIT
AT STARBUCKS."

I have
a healthy
self image
despite what
I look like on
FaceTime.

MANTRA FOR GPS

Imagine taking an endless back road to nowhere . . .
Because your GPS said you'd save 3 minutes if you got off the highway.
In front of you, notice a bright yellow
school bus making infinite stops.
Feel a rush of regret surge through your chakras,
as you are guided on a journey of continuous right turns.

How do you feel?
Like you've been driving around in circles?
Simply surrender to the soothing, slightly condescending
voice of your GPS.
She is leading you toward a gleaming bridge, over an
unknown body of water.
When you've reached the middle of the bridge, allow your
fingernails to dig into the steering wheel.
Slowly, become aware that your GPS has lost its signal.
Notice how she begins to free-associate:
"Go left/go right/take the roundabout/make a U-turn."
And relax as she recalculates . . .
Sending you through city traffic at rush hour.

As our journey reaches its final destination,
honor your anxiety by honking at a red light to make it turn green.
And now, let it go.
Today, we discover Modern Mantra #2 . . .

"I AM POWERLESS OVER MY GPS."

Today,
I will resist
"reply all."

MANTRA FOR THE MALL

Feel yourself floating up the escalator of
a suburban cathedral.
Behold the pure white light; the peaceful
tinkle of a fountain; the serene background music.

At this very moment in time . . .
Twenty minutes before rush hour starts . . .
There is nowhere on Earth you would less like to be.
But you need to return a complicated scarf
someone gave you from Banana Republic.

Channel your spirit animal, the majestic mall rat.
See yourself scurry past the mall-walkers to a
towering store directory.
Gaze in awe at the billions and billions of stores . . .
And ponder how it is possible that you still have no
idea how to get to Banana Republic.

As you feel the first wave of mall fatigue
washing over you,
breathe in through the nostrils.
Breathe in the Auntie Anne's soft pretzel air . . .
The Crabtree & Evelyn seaside room-spray air . . .
The Bath & Body Works vanilla face mask air.

With each breath, feel yourself losing focus . . .
Surrendering to your inner consumer . . .
Wandering aimlessly around H&M with a
soft pretzel in your mouth.

Slowly, find yourself sitting in a giant,
vibrating chair at the entrance of Brookstone.
Try not to question how you wound up here . . .
Simply be in the moment.
And when the moment is over . . .
Simply be in Foot Locker, getting a new pair
of tennis sneakers in case you decide
to learn how to play tennis one day.

Whenever you start dying inside, envision
what your credit card bill is going to look like
this month.
Abruptly, envision yourself stuck in rush
hour traffic.
In your trunk lies an abundance of purchases
you had no intention of buying.
On your passenger seat sits a complicated
scarf from Banana Republic you forgot to return.
Today, we are reminded of Modern Mantra #3 . . .

"I AM A LASER-FOCUSED MALL WARRIOR."

I am
learning
to accept
Alexa for
who she is.

MANTRA FOR GLUTEN INTOLERANCE

Visualize ravioli.
Inhale its doughy energies . . .
And drift off to a healing space, such as a bathroom or
emergency room, where you will wind up if you eat it.

Now, let a new image materialize.
It is a lovely evening and you are dining out with companions.
Hear yourself dialoguing with the waitress . . .
Notice how she rolls her eyes when you ask if the rice noodles are
boiled in the same water as the ravioli.
Feel your face chakra radiate the crimson glow of gluten-free shame.
And release with a sip of your nasty hard cider.

Now, envision your companions sharing a delicious
pitcher of wheat beer.
Flow into forced-smile pose.
Honor your food envy as you evoke their meal:

Thick-crust pizza . . .
Soft flour tortillas . . .
Warm bread pudding . . .

Our voyage of gluten intolerance now turns inward,
as we bring the focus back to our own food.
Become one with your gluten-free cookie.
Bask in its gummy, sandy aura.
Do not become destabilized if you experience an urge
to spit it out and chug the entire pitcher of wheat beer.
Rather, reclaim your powers of digestion with Modern Mantra # 4 . . .

"I AM A WHEAT-FREE, BARLEY-FREE, RYE-FREE, GLUTEN FREEDOM FIGHTER."

I release
the guilt of
not sponsoring
my colleague's
cousin in the
walkathon.

MANTRA FOR AN OPEN-PLAN OFFICE

Clear your mind and transport yourself to a place with no walls . . .
No barriers . . .
No personal space whatsoever between you . . .
And the insufferable co-worker next to you.
Sense that he is so close that he's basically sitting in your lap . . .
So very close that you can hear each breath he takes . . .
And you can also smell it.
Inhale deeply through your nasal pathways,
and gag on the sardines he is eating straight out of the tin . . .
While he talks to his doctor on speakerphone.
Let your familiar queasiness wash over you,
as you absorb each word of his conversation:
Ingrown hair . . .
Drained abscess . . .
Skin tag . . .
Now, take a moment to turn your focus to the *click, click, click*
from the high-intensity keyboard typist on the other side of you.
And the chronic cough from the contagious colleague behind you.
Feel yourself finally composing your letter of resignation . . .
Though you do not have one single job prospect to fall back on.
Ready to hit Send?
Stop.
Reframe your rage and repeat Modern Mantra #5 . . .

"I AM AN OPEN FLOWER WHO BLOSSOMS IN AN OPEN FLOOR PLAN."

I practice
patience when
my parents
ask me for
tech support.

MANTRA FOR AIRPORT SECURITY

Stand frozen in place for a count of forty-five minutes.
Bring to mind a magnificent metal detector far in the distance.
At the front of the line, picture a guy who thought he could take
his toolbox as a carry-on.
Sense the last vestiges of compassion slowly being sucked from your soul.

Now, transcend the chaos and confusion that surrounds you.
Raise your head and look heavenward . . .
Let your ears embrace a divine message from above.
It is the gate attendant, announcing that your flight has begun boarding.

Resist getting stuck in a bad thought loop.
Instead, see yourself reaching out to a TSA officer . . .
And being ignored while he whisks a family of five to the front,
with their emotional support labradoodle.
Pause to let your inner critic ask you why you still haven't enrolled in TSA Pre.

At last, we approach the magnificent metal detector.
Like Buddha, we surrender our material possessions . . .
And we place them in a gray plastic bin.
See yourself walking through the gateway to freedom . . .
And being randomly selected for a full-body pat-down.

And now, envision your aircraft gently floating higher and higher . . .
Into the clear blue sky . . .
Without you.

Through clenched teeth, we mutter Modern Mantra #6 . . .

"I WILL NOT BECOME A SECURITY THREAT ON THE AIRPORT SECURITY LINE."

Yes I CAN
find the
end of the
masking tape.

MANTRA FOR WHOLE FOODS

Slip into a vegetative state and become
an avocado.
You are an organic, Ayurvedic, sustainably
sourced, non-GMO, hormone-free, grass-fed,
pole-caught, fair trade, holistic, inclusive,
expensive avocado.
And you are not manufactured in a facility
that also processes peanuts.
Sense yourself being studied . . .
And then squeezed . . .
And, finally, sniffed . . .
By a customer robed in Lululemon.
She has inconsiderately parked her shopping
cart in the middle of the aisle . . .
And illegally parked her Range Rover
in a handicapped space.

Now, leave the avocado self and return to
the human self.
Express gratitude that you are not really
an avocado.
You're just having a stress-induced episode
at Whole Foods.

As you continue losing touch with the real
world, let the song of the
sirens seduce you into a sea of pure, white milk.
Drown in an ocean of options . . .
Hemp milk . . .
Pea milk . . .
Cashew milk . . .

We pause here for a moment of
mindfulness, and contemplate how they even
get milk out of all that stuff.
And now, we reclaim mindlessness,
and fling each type of milk into our cart.
Along with grape seed oil, stevia extract, and
shampoo free of sodium laureth sulfate.
And a loofah sponge.

Slowly, bring your conscious attention
to the self-righteous shoppers who
surround you.
Pay special attention to a hipster dad
sampling vegan beef jerky.
Notice the irony of his leather jacket . . .
Feel the force of his free-range parenting
style, as his six-year-old pelts you with
hydroponic grape tomatoes.

With intention, spread your wings and fly
like a bird to bulk foods.

See yourself standing erect, your hands
raised high above your head.
Reach higher and higher, to a crystal
clear container of chia seeds . . .
And watch them cascade like a waterfall
all over the floor.

We close with a past-life regression.
Picture yourself at the check-out counter.
Whilst the cashier spends 45 minutes bubble-
wrapping your blueberries, let your mind drift
back to your life long ago.
A life before you spent twelve dollars on
satsuma tangerines,
and you happily subsisted on Ramen and Pringles.
Hear the rumblings of an existential crisis draw
closer, and closer.
And now, break free of the past.
We proudly embrace our beautiful bougie-ness
with Modern Mantra #7 . . .

"I TOSS MY FIRST WORLD PROBLEMS INTO A WHOLE FOODS TOTE BAG."

Preparing
my taxes
gives me a
deep sense
of purpose.

MANTRA FOR INSTAGRAM

Tune out the noise of the day and visualize two beautiful persons
deeply in love, greeting you from their tropical vacation.
Feel your feelings:

Jealousy.
Envy.
Inadequacy.

Let's scroll deeper through your Instagram feed, fixing your third
eye on the kiwi smoothie your friend had for breakfast today.
If you find yourself feeling food-shamed, simply scroll.
Turn your gaze to the selfie from your friends at the spa.
Quiet the questions cluttering your aura, such as:

"What filter did they use to make their teeth so white?"
"Did she get Botox?"
"Do they ever work?"

Instead, tap into the *positive* energies of all the Likes . . .
From all their friends . . .
And wonder why *you* don't have as many followers as they do.

As we wrap ourselves in a blanket of self-loathing, what can we
do to restore our #serenity . . .
And break the toxic cycle of comparing ourselves to others?
We can *unfollow* them, right?
Wrong.
Presently, we repeat Modern Mantra #8 . . .

"I AM INSPIRED BY THE PERFECT LIVES I SEE ON INSTAGRAM."

The
porta potty
makes me
stronger.

MANTRA FOR PUBLIC TRANSPORTATION

Embark on a rush-hour journey of
sensory stimulation.
As you summon your subway, awaken
your sense of touch.
Feel a crowd of commuters shoving you
off the platform
and through the closing doors.
Once inside, notice your sense of touch
intensifying when your pole-mate's backpack
begins to pummel you.
Own your sense of touch by allowing
yourself to mentally jab him with your elbow.

Next we awaken our sense of sight.
Offer a look of disgust to a passenger
who is clipping her nails.
Stay present as you watch a stray fingernail
float through the air like a feather, gently
landing on your lap.
Find the courage to remove this fingernail,
and let go into a warm sea of hand sanitizer.
Take a moment to marvel at those who
practice personal hygiene in public places.

Inhale through flared nostrils for a count of four.
Your sense of *smell* is now aroused, drawn to a
noxious sandwich being eaten nearby.

Activate your sense of *taste* to savor the flavors.
Tuna fish . . .
Egg salad . . .
Meatballs . . .
Release all thoughts of being repelled
by humanity.
Simply sit in silent judgment.

Whenever you feel your subway slowing
to a standstill in a subterranean tunnel,
anoint your sense of hearing.
Try to tune in to an incomprehensible
announcement coming from the loudspeakers.
Reflect upon any random words you are
able to make out over the static. . .

Disabled train . . .
Signal malfunction . . .
Indefinite delay . . .

Our subway sensorium concludes with breathwork.
Take a series of shallow, choking breaths
accompanied by difficulty swallowing. And now,
banish your pending panic attack with the
cathartic power of Modern Mantra #9. . .

"THE SUBWAY EXHILARATES MY SENSES."

I live my
best life with
only limited
guidance
from Yelp.

MANTRA FOR AIRBNB

Form an image of a spacious, Zen-like loft, flowing with feng shui energies.
Feel your finger clicking on the reservations link . . .
See yourself swinging open the door . . .
Find yourself in a place that looks nothing like it did on the website.

If you catch yourself backtracking in disillusionment, simply breathe.
Follow the stale air to a bright red plastic cup, brimming with cigarette butts.
Notice your allergy center becoming activated . . .
Begin to connect deeply with your renter's remorse.

Now, envision the kitchen.
Sense yourself becoming buoyant with hope, drawn like a magnet
to a stainless-steel dishwasher.
Go ahead . . . open it.
An abundance of dishes awaits you within . . .
Bedazzled in egg yolk and spaghetti sauce.

Whenever you are ready, bravely face the bedroom.
Choose to not see the dead housefly pressed against the window glass.
Choose instead to bathe in the light.
First the red light . . .
Then the blue light . . .
Then the flashing white headlights, all from the squad cars at
the police station across the street.
Let a piercing symphony of sirens lead you to an epiphany:
For *this* is what the online listing meant by "extremely safe neighborhood."

Finally, form a vision of yourself at a laptop.
Feel yourself transforming your suffering into revenge . . .
And allow yourself to mentally compose the scathing review
you are going to post about this place.
Now, let it go.
Bring acceptance to your dystopian dwelling with Modern Mantra #10. . .

"I HAVE BEEN SENT TO THIS AIRBNB FOR A REASON."

43

I step on
a Lego
barefoot,
yet I do
not fall.

MANTRA FOR HOT YOGA

Visualize doing Mountain Pose on a
snow-capped peak in Siberia.
Your fingers, exquisitely numb with frostbite . . .
Your teeth, clanking together in a
sublime shiver . . .
Your nervous system, entering a
blissful state of hypothermia.

Now, acknowledge that you are
not actually in Siberia.
You are in a hot yoga class, but the
heat has made you delusional.
Inhale the effluvium.
Feet . . .
Underarms . . .
Clammy yoga blocks that may or may not
have been sanitized since the hairy guy from
the last class had them between his legs.

As you flow into Perspiration Pose, place an
imaginary yoga strap around your heal and
stretch toward the scorching sun.
As you stretch, reflect upon whose foot the
strap was wrapped around before yours.

Was it the foot with bunions a couple rows
ahead of you?
The foot with yellowing toenails to your left?
Close your eyes and give yourself permission
to never open them again until class is over.

Slowly and catatonically, flow into
Heat Stroke Pose.
Practice self-compassion by transforming
your yoga mat into a stretcher.
Lying flat on your back, form a vision of
firefighters rushing in to hose you down.

Finally, flow into Downward Dehydrated Dog.
Visualize yourself on all fours, your mouth open
wide, your tongue fully extended.
Notice the panting rhythm of your breath . . .
And now, roll over and play dead.

With Shavasana, we chant Modern Mantra #11 . . .

"I CHOOSE COLD YOGA."

The gift of getting laid off provides endless time for my mindfulness practice.

MANTRA FOR A SMARTPHONE

Today's mantra is for those moments when we become triggered by our hand-held device. Let's begin by mentally unlocking it with our fingerprint ID, pressing over . . .
and over . . . and over . . .
Because the fingerprint thing hasn't worked since we tried to update our operating system.

Think back to a time long ago when you still remembered your password.
4793?
Try again.
4937?
Try again.
And again . . .
And again . . .
And again.
How are you feeling?
Displeased?

Restore your Chi with a soothing selection from your music library.

What do you hear?
Nothing?
That is because your playlist has been mysteriously deleted . . .
Along with a dozen contacts . . .
And an email that has somehow gotten stuck in your outbox.
Did you even know you *had* an outbox?
You do.
But you will never be able to find it.

Slowly, imagine losing your wireless connection . . .
And then losing your battery power . . .
And finally, losing your mind.

And now, open your eyes and hold your device to your heart,
as you chant Modern Mantra #12 . . .

"I FORGIVE MY SMARTPHONE."

I transform the 3am chirp of my broken smoke alarm into the peaceful song of the nightbird.

MANTRA FOR TINDER

The prophets teach us there is a soulmate for each being on earth.
Right now, begin the process of elimination.
Start by visualizing a soulmate who is posing suggestively with a boa constrictor.
Feel a surge of strength rush through your index finger . . .
And allow it to swiftly swipe this soulmate to the left.
Now, form an image of an outdoorsy soulmate whose face is concealed
in all five photos by mirrored sunglasses and a bicycle helmet.
Feel yourself slowly falling into a vortex of soulmates.
Enter a trance-like state of swiping, and let the teachings of
the prophet Béyonce be your guide . . .

To the left . . . to the left . . . to the left . . .

As we intensify our guided soulmate search, we learn to let go
of toxic perfectionism.
Really let go.
Try to envision an imaginary horizontal bar floating high atop
your soulmate's profile picture.
The bar symbolizes your standards.
Using all the force of your being, lower the bar.
Lower the bar as low as it can possibly go.
When the bar cannot go any lower, set yourself free and swipe to the right.

Swipe right for the "30ish" soulmate who looks suspiciously like a 65ish soulmate.
Swipe right for the soulmate who is searching for a "Committed, NSA relationship."
Swipe right for the soulmate whose bio says *"do me."*

And now the time has come to manifest a soulmate Match.
See yourself stalking your soulmate Match on social media . . .
And discovering that your soulmate Match already has a soulmate match . . .
And their 20th anniversary pictures are all over Facebook.

As we delete the app for the third time this year, we recite Modern Mantra #13 . . .

"I PRACTICE SELF-LOVE BY SWIPING LEFT."

I do not
have the thing
I just read
about on
WebMD.

MANTRA FOR THE MULTIPLEX

Flow into a space where fantasy unfolds
before your eyes.
Keep flowing into that space while the
coming attractions start, because you can't
find anywhere to sit.
With each step you take, visualize that
you're walking on a trail.
Hear the crunch of filthy popcorn kernels
beneath your feet . . .
And the squeak of your shoes on a stream
of spilled Coke.

Be unafraid of the darkness.
Trust that the trail will lead to its source . . .
A very tall spectator who will be sitting in front of
you for the next 120 minutes.

Gradually, allow an image to form
of this spectator.
Perhaps the spectator you're imagining has
brought his toddlers along, even though the movie
is rated R for violence and nudity . . .
Perhaps your spectator is eating Cheez Whiz
nachos with his mouth open . . .
Perhaps—no, definitely—your spectator is talking
on his cellphone during the reminder to
silence all cellphones.

Breathe in, and feel yourself being swept up
by a poignant scene.
Breathe out, and reimagine that scene with
added sound effects . . .

The *annoying* sound of the spectator slurping
his supersized Coke.
The *disturbing* sound of the spectator telling
his children which character he thinks will get
murdered next.
The *aggravating* sound of the spectator telling no
one in particular that the actress looks like that one
who used to play Buffy the Vampire Slayer.

As the spectator continues his blow-by-blow
commentary, take a moment to ponder his
spiritual significance.
Acknowledge that he could be a guru who has
been placed here to guide your
motion-picture vision quest . . .
And affirm that you didn't pay ten bucks on
Fandango to sit behind a guru.

The climax of our motion picture meditation
is a confrontation scene.
Inhale deeply, and feel yourself leaning closer and
closer to the spectator seated in front of you . . .
Form an image of your mouth placed ever so
closely to his ear . . .
And with the force of a tornado, exhale to
produce an explosive noise:
Shhhhhhhhhhhhhhhhhhhhhhhhhhhhhhhhhhhhh.

Now, resume your practice of seeing the good in
all persons, via Modern Mantra #14 . . .

"THE SCHMUCK AT THE CINEMA SHINES WITH SELF-EXPRESSION."

I didn't cause
the paper jam.
I can't control
the paper jam.
I will heal from
the paper jam.

MANTRA FOR CUSTOMER SERVICE

Tap into the excruciating sound of
Air Supply's "I'm All Out of Love," wafting
from your speakerphone.
When you are prompted, please press or
say one for billing, two for sales, three for
technical support, four for account
management, and so on until you have
attained a heightened sense of hostility.
And now, find your voice . . .
Notice your voice repeating the same word,
over and over.
"Representative."
"Representative."
"REPRESENTATIVE!"

Slowly, feel yourself becoming connected,
truly *connected,* to an actual human being.
And then to another one because you have
reached the wrong department.
And another . . . and another . . . and another.

As day turns to night, our journey quest for
customer service moves past grief to a
place of hope.

Imagine becoming connected to a
Relationship Manager.
She is here to support you . . .
And reassure you . . .
And ask you for your five-digit verification
access PIN.

What if you told her you don't have one?
Visualize a harmonious world where your
customer servant practices empathy and
kindness. And then return to reality.
Listen as she passive-aggressively apologizes
that she is not authorized to assist customers
who claim they don't have a five-digit verification access PIN.

We complete today's meditation by demanding
to speak to a supervisor.
Gently circle back to "All Out of Love" on your
speakerphone . . .
Continue to hold for a count of eternity.
Whenever you are suspiciously disconnected,
recite Modern Mantra #15 . . .

"I WILL NOT BE TRIGGERED BY THE CUSTOMER SERVICE REPRESENTATIVE."

I am
the Yin to
the Yang of
the sidewalk
texter who
slammed
into me.

MANTRA FOR A JUICE CLEANSE

Relax your gag reflex and manifest a mouth-watering meal of kale and cabbage juice.
Allow your taste buds to savor the flavors . . .
Hints of dirt . . .
Notes of sticks . . .
Undertones of socks . . .
Today is the first day of the rest of your juice cleanse.

Slowly, and with a distinct lack of enthusiasm, imagine a second day of your juice cleanse.
You are swallowing a tempting luncheon of cauliflower-beet-acai.
Notice your teeth becoming coated with a slimy film . . .
And your poop being brightened by a scary red tint that turns out to be beets when you diagnose it on WebMD.

With every $8 bottle of cucumber-chlorophyll-kombucha you choke down, sense the toxins and impurities leaving your body . . .
And the pleasure leaving your body . . .
And the vast amount of pee leaving your body . . .

If at any point you notice yourself becoming a bit listless, unfocused, or clinically depressed, fight the temptation to fill your void with food.
Rather, unleash the juice cleanser's code of conduct:
See yourself smile-lying about how *energized* you feel since you started your cleanse.

As we go deeper on our juice cleanse journey, try your very hardest to visualize even the most remote possibility of a third day.
Bring awareness to a pounding migraine in your crown chakra from lack of caffeine . . .
And an embarrassing growl in your stomach chakra from lack of everything else.

To heal these imbalances, we culminate with a sense memory exercise.
Tap into the memory of chewing.
Begin by opening your mouth, and proceed by closing it.
Continue this pattern for a count of three:
Open, close . . .
Open, close . . .
Open, insert Dunkin' Donut, chant Modern Mantra #16 . . .

"TODAY,
I RECLAIM
SOLIDS."

I practice restraint in my use of emojis.

MANTRA FOR SELFIE-DEFENSE

Visualize meandering on a hillside path
ablaze with wildflowers.
Now, visualize meandering into a person who's
blocking the path while she takes a selfie.
Feel your arms crossing in a tightly wound
display of irritation.
Add a rhythmic, annoyed tapping of your
foot, as she takes another one with a bouquet
of colorful coneflowers.
And another making a duck face . . .
And another with tousled hair arranged into a
beachy, "I woke up this way" look.

Take a deep breath of disbelief and imagine
her posting each image on her infinite array
of social media platforms . . .
While she continues to block the path.
Bring attention to your tongue.
Hear it making a *tsk* sound at her.
Whenever you are ready, give yourself
permission to meander past her in a huff,
perhaps with an exaggerated stomp of
the feet for emphasis.

As you continue meandering, follow the path
to the peak of a magnificent mountain.

When you have triumphantly meandered to
the top of the mountain, behold the view:
a scenic group of tourists gathered around
a selfie stick.

Be still and connect with their supreme
sense of cluelessness.
Become perversely fascinated by the fact that
they are not even *trying* to get the breathtaking
view into their picture, but are absorbed instead
by their special selfie hand gestures:

The horizontal peace sign . . .
The thumbs-up . . .
The hang-ten.

We close our meditation with an act of catharsis.
Form an image of marching over to the tour
group and snatching their selfie stick.
Feel the strength of a Shaolin monk as you
mindfully crack it over your knee and break
it in half.

Gradually, bring yourself back to the
present moment.
Resume meandering while muttering
Modern Mantra #17 . . .

"I WALK IN PEACE AMONGST INCESSANT SELFIE-TAKERS."

This is
the year I
change all my
passwords.

MANTRA FOR DIY

Sit comfortably on a celestial toilet.
Allow your mind to explore each nuance and
nook of the bathroom that envelopes you.
The outdated fixtures . . .
The depressing color . . .
The unflattering lights.

As you explore each nuance and nook,
begin to actualize your lavatory's
metamorphosis into a spa-like sanctuary.
Feel yourself slipping into a deep,
delusional state . . .
And believe that you can Do It Yourself.

Slowly, form an image of Yourself trying to
unscrew an old, leaky showerhead.
Firstly with a wrench . . .
Then with pliers . . .
Then with a hammer you use to smash
it off in a maniacal rage.

With a restorative in-breath, envision a new,
oversized Rainforest Showerhead you
manifested from Bed, Bath & Beyond.
And with a profanity-laced out-breath,
become keenly aware that it's way too big
for your shower.
Feel yourself detaching from the rational mind . . .
Harnessing your frustration to *force* the
fixture onto the pipe.

Pause to reflect upon how you're going
to explain all the scratches when you try
to return it.

Now, take leave of this image and form
a new one.
You are a masterful artist, standing before
the canvas that is your bathroom.
You are behatted in a French beret . . .
And you are holding a palette of free paint
swatches from Home Depot.

Barely Beige . . .
Colorless Cream . . .
Neutral Nothing . . .

Be mindful not to rush your creative process . . .
Because the spackling alone is going to
take the whole weekend.
And now, set your inner artist free to mentally
paint your bathroom.
And to mentally repaint it when your inner artist
realizes the color looks totally different than it
did on the swatch.

Today, we awaken from our DIY fever dream to
call a professional.
Today, we chant Modern Mantra #18 . . .

"I WILL
BE SORRY
IF I DO IT
MYSELF."

The
robocalls
will not send
me into a
rage spiral.

MANTRA FOR CHUCK E. CHEESE'S

Release all serenity and let your inner child
run rampant.
Notice your inner child's eyes blurring from
a barrage of flashing video monitors . . .
Put your inner child at risk of early hearing loss
from piercing sirens and deafening bells . . .
Take your inner child to a hellish dreamscape
of visual and auditory assault.

Now, bring attention to a violent arcade game
your inner child demands to play.
Visualize your inner child's little hands clutching
a greasy steering wheel . . .
And careening through an apocalyptic
streetscape on the screen.
Feel your inner child fully engaged in the pure,
innocent wonder of vehicular combat.

Gradually, become aware that the game is broken,
and is not dispensing the tickets your inner
child will need to get a prize.
Feel your jaw locking in tension . . .
And be present as your inner child has a tantrum.

Our spiritual practice empowers us to
transform rage into resilience.
Impart that resilience by promising your inner
child a sausage pizza if it stops crying.
And also a side of wings.
And Dippin' Dots ice cream.
And a sippy cup of Mountain Dew.

If at any point you sense that you
are exposing your inner child to food-borne
pathogens, simply acknowledge this is a
self-judging thought.

Now, reorient yourself to the present play space.
Imagine your inner child watching a mother scream
at her son for throwing Skee-Balls at his sister . . .
And a toddler picking her nose and wiping it on
the *Temple Run* trackball . . .
And a baby getting stuck in an enclosed
climbing tube.

Whenever you feel that your inner child has
reached a heightened state of sensory overload,
manifest the appearance of a mythical figure
who is part man and part mouse.
As if in a bad hallucination, envision the
creature doing a live musical performance for
your inner child . . .
And for a mob of other inner children who
swarm him for selfies and fight for prize tickets
that fall from the sky like confetti.

Finally, give yourself permission to abandon
your inner child.
As you run for the exit, slow down and recite
Modern Mantra #19 . . .

"I WILL NOT HAVE AN EXISTENTIAL CRISIS AT CHUCK E. CHEESE'S."

I am honored that my coworker valued my idea enough to steal it.

MANTRA FOR INSOMNIA

Recline on a mattress at two o'clock in the morning—your eyes wide open and fixed on the ceiling.
Gradually, allow a vision to form of a spot on the ceiling.
Feel yourself growing preoccupied with the spot . . .
Scrutinize the spot . . .
Perseverate on it from each and every angle.
Dwell in the possibility that the spot means there's a leak in your roof, and the ceiling could come crashing down in your sleep.

After one hour of ceiling focus, imagine gently pressing a pillow over your face chakra.
Calm your active mind with the pure, childlike ritual of counting sheep.
When you reach a count of three-and-a-half sheep, notice that you are unable to count any more sheep because you are too busy counting the reasons you can't sleep.
Was it the coffee? The ice cream?
Why did you eat ice cream when you are trying to lose weight?
Was it the wine? The workout? The non-drowsy Claritin?
Or is it possible . . .
Even probable . . .
That you have sleep apnea.

In hour two of our all-night meditation, visualize googling sleep apnea to see what it even is.

Absorb the ethereal blue light of your screen.
Slowly, become conscious that you heard somewhere that blue light causes insomnia.
Give yourself permission to google "blue light insomnia" to see if this is true . . .
And feel a surge of unwanted energy when you find out it is.
Envision channeling that energy into Amazon.com, and harnessing it to buy melatonin . . .
And also to do some holiday shopping.
Now, channel that energy into a Netflix binge . . .
And finally into Facebook, so you can search for your high school prom date.

If at any point you experience a sense of impending doom because you have to get up for work soon, stay in the present moment.
Imagine you are a beautiful butterfly, fluttering away from the fears that keep you awake at night.
Flutter away from the fear that you will not be able to afford an assisted living facility when you turn 90 . . .
Flutter away from the fear that someone could be trying to steal your identity . . .
Flutter away from the fear that your health insurance will not cover your sleep apnea.

Once you have fluttered yourself into a cold sweat, greet the dawning of a new day with Modern Mantra #20 . . .

"I AM NOT SLEEPLESS, I AM TIRELESS."

Today is
the day I
stop saying
"wackadoodle."

MANTRA FOR CROWDFUNDING

Today we turn our mindfulness practice
away from the self . . .
And towards the CD our neighbor's rich
nephew wants to record with our money.
Begin by visualizing an e-mail for the
nephew's Kickstarter campaign.
Perhaps the nephew is in crisis because he
needs more studio space . . .
And he is suffering because he wants
another amp.
If you had to walk a mile in the nephew's
shoes, what would you do?
Get a job?

Gradually, notice an unexpected pang of
guilt gnawing within you . . .
By aiding others, according to the tenets of
karma, you will get precious gifts in return.
For a twenty-five-dollar donation, you will get
an autographed copy of the nephew's CD.
And for fifty, you will get a free house concert.

Bring awareness to the fact that you very much
wish not to get either of these gifts.

As you begin to question just how selfish
of a human being you are,
Find yourself clicking on the nephew's
Battle of the Bands video . . .
Even though you should really be doing
your taxes.
Hear the unbearable screech of the
nephew's electric guitar . . .
And the unpleasant nasal tone of his vocals.

As his video comes to completion, visualize
the nephew reaching out to you in an
earnest pitch for support.
His arms extended . . .
His open palms cupped together . . .
His wrist sheathed in a $1,500 Apple Watch.

Presently, we chant Modern Mantra #21 . . .

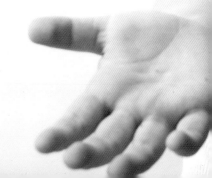

"I AM BENEVOLENT THOUGH I BLOW OFF THE KICKSTARTER CAMPAIGN."

Spending $26 on razor blades enriches my practice of self-care.

MANTRA FOR A BAD WEDDING

Pull back the curtain to a nondescript
catering hall.
See yourself seated at a table for all the B-list
guests who do not know each other.
Take a breath of unventilated air.
If you sense yourself becoming distracted
by a deafening thud, or thump, simply
acknowledge that it is the sound of "Louie,
Louie" being played at one of the other
weddings upstairs . . .
And return your focus to the ragtag guests
at your table:
The bride's Soul Cycle instructor . . .
The groom's Austrian host family from junior
year abroad . . .
An elderly couple who grew up with
somebody's grandparents.

Go deep and search for something to talk about.
Note a sense of hopelessness gnawing at
your core . . .
And a thirst growing inside you.
Now, free yourself to quench that thirst
at the bar.

What do you notice about it?
That it is a cash bar?
That you do not have cash, and the bartender
won't let you Venmo a vodka tonic?

Like a river, let yourself flow . . .
Let the current carry your consciousness to a DJ
wearing a tuxedo T-shirt and sunglasses.
Hear the sound of his voice mispronouncing
the names of each family member he calls
to the stage . . .
And the sound of his boom box blaring a
never-ending loop of The Electric Slide.

We consummate our wedding meditation
with a chicken cutlet.
And a medley of boiled carrot cubes.
Imagine choking down each rubbery morsel
on your dinner plate.
Pause to ponder how much longer you
can survive this most joyous of occasions.
And now, speak Modern Mantra #22 or
forever hold your peace . . .

"I AM AN ANGEL AT THE WEDDING FROM HELL."

I can conquer the self-scanning lane.

MANTRA FOR MULTITASKING

Awaken to the simplicity of a morning
mindfulness walk.
Drink in the sunrise . . .
And sip on a smoothie so you can have
breakfast at the same time.
Listen to the sound of the gentle breeze
rustling through the willows . . .
And a podcast you downloaded while getting
dressed and checking Twitter.
Take in the call of the songbird . . .
Whilst taking a call from your mother on your
headset.

Should you feel your focus scattering as you
mindfully walk and have breakfast and listen
to a podcast and talk to your mother,
Simply allow your mother's voice to fade
into the background.
Maintain awareness that she is saying
some words, but neutralize those words into
white noise . . .
And free yourself to simultaneously gaze at a
stream of YouTube videos flowing through your
smart watch . . .
As your wrist pulsates with push notifications.

Gradually, set forth to *enhance* your
mindfulness walk.
Imagine quickening your pace to add
a cardio component . . .
Manifest a pet dog you are holding on a leash . . .
And a baby you are pushing in a jogging stroller.
Or twins, which would enable you to raise two
children concurrently.

Once you have enhanced your mindfulness walk
into a mindfulness *run*, become aware of a
powerful, somewhat compulsive need to
enhance it even more.
Infuse your mindfulness run with a
sense of *purpose*.
Look inward—perhaps while stretching or jogging in place—and ask, "Where am I running *to*?"

Slowly, allow a vision of Jiffy Lube to form.
You have mindfully run here to pick up your car.
See yourself seated serenely in the waiting area,
making the most of this singular moment
by calling JetBlue to find out how to use your
frequent flier miles.
Know, intuitively, that the approximate hold time
will be fifteen minutes . . .
And enhance that hold time with some mental
mobile banking.

We bring closure to our mindfulness run by
enhancing it into a mindfulness drive.
Visualize your journey home from Jiffy Lube.
Listen to the road beneath your wheels . . .
And an NPR interview, a classic rock station, a
stand-up act on satellite radio, and an audiobook.
And the haunting, high-pitched siren of the
police car behind you.

As you are pulled over for texting while
driving, enhance your experience with Modern
Mantra #23 . . .

"I MULTITASK IN MODERATION"

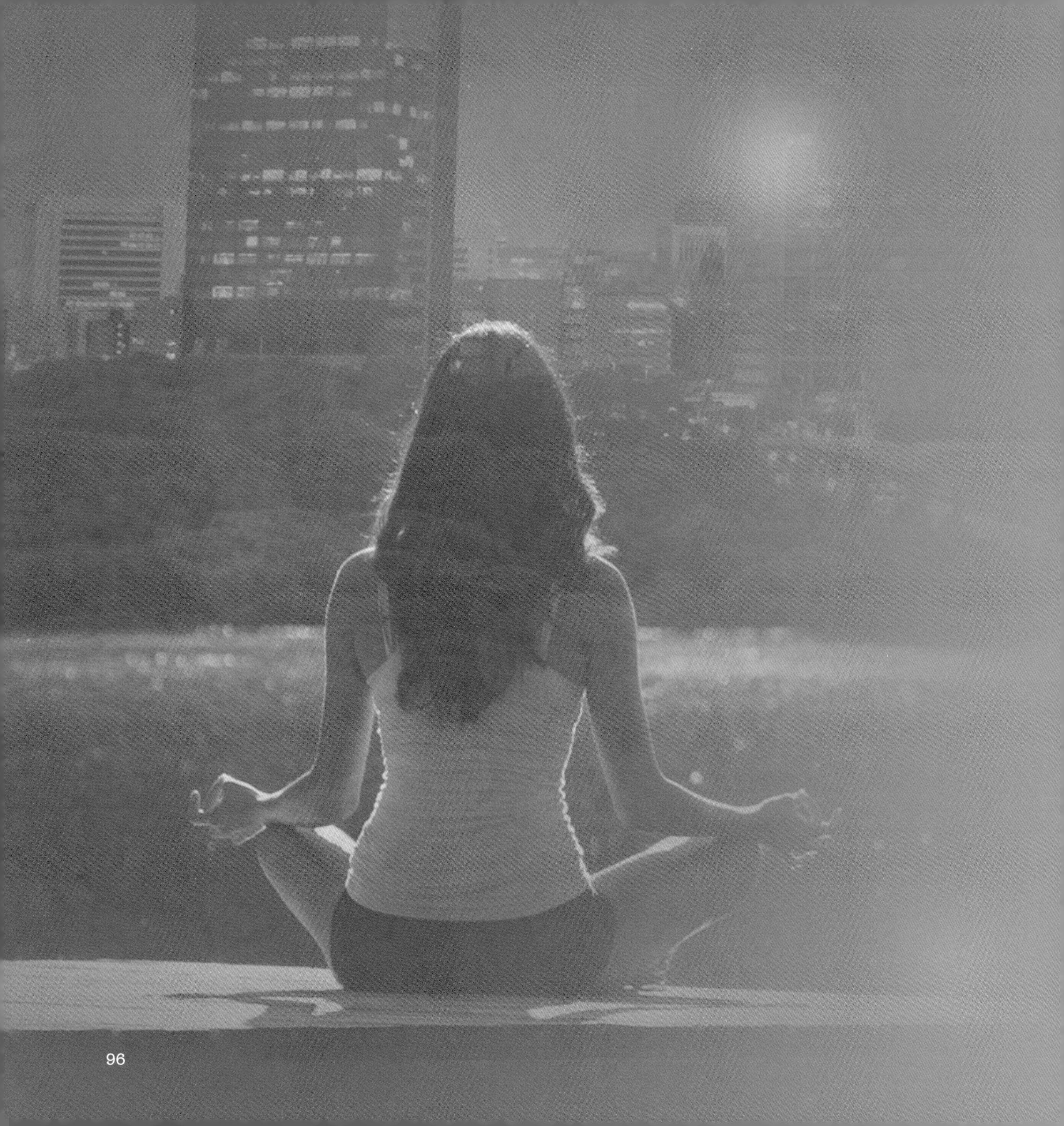

I am on
a journey
to find the
Unsubscribe
button.

MANTRA FOR THE GYM

Relax and go to a place to lose your belly fat . . .
And your dignity.
Experience a surge of self-consciousness as
you do public donkey kicks . . .
Activate your fight-or-flight reflex when a
creep in sweatbands asks you to hold his
feet for sit-ups.

On this journey of body positivity, resist
comparing yourself to the many, many
persons who are far, far fitter than you.
Instead, compare yourself to the Chair Yoga
students who took the shuttle bus here
from the nursing home.

Give yourself permission to gaze into the
mirrors you've been trying to ignore.
Who do you see in the reflection?

A trainer, Snapchatting his six-pack?
A worker, wiping down the glass with Windex?

As you swing a rainbow-colored kettlebell,
experience a rush of endorphins in your
energy center.
And a sharp, stabbing sensation in your
rotator cuff.

We conclude with a cool-down visualization.
Picture yourself on a treadmill.
See yourself walking and walking . . .
Walking until the light inside of you has died.
And now, practice positive self-talk.
With every step you take, simply repeat
Modern Mantra #24 . . .

"I WILL NOT LOSE MY WILL TO LIVE AT THE GYM"

I see
sunshine
through a
cloud of
secondhand
vape.

MANTRA FOR UBER

Access a time from your past when you were
pelted with pouring rain while trying to
hail a cab.
Feel the breeze of each taxi rushing by you,
misting you with a spray of filthy puddle water.
Slowly, tap into a sensation of being invisible.
And now, remember you have the Uber app.

Go ahead and click the app.
Give yourself some contemplative space to
wonder why it's taking so long to load.
Be mindful of each unique raindrop as it drips
onto your screen and potentially causes
irreversible damage.
Slowly, allow a series of words to take
shape on your wet screen . . .
Surge Pricing in Effect.

Say no to negativity . . .
And say yes to paying five times the normal fare.
Try not to dwell on that which cannot
be known . . .
Such as what the normal fare even is . . .
Rather, express gratitude for the abundance of
unclear options available to you:

*Uber X, UberXL, UberSelect, UberBlack,
UberPool* . . .

As we arrive at the midpoint of our meditation,
we bring awareness to the fact that we are
still not within our Uber after a half hour,
even though the app said we'd be picked
up in four minutes.
Bring forth to your screen a tiny,
ebony rectangle.
See it inching closer and closer to your
pulsating point on the GPS map.
Concentrate on the rectangle as it drives
straight past you.
And then watch the rectangle backing down
a one-way street to retrieve you at last.

Breathe the musk-scented air . . .
Hear the deafening drum solo . . .
Notice your driver speeding recklessly in
a bus lane while yelling at his girlfriend
on speakerphone.

And now, tighten your seat belt and chant
Modern Mantra #25 . . .

"I WILL FIND THE JOY IN MY UBER JOURNEY."

The death
of my ATM card's
magnetic strip
teaches me to
live each day to
the fullest.

MANTRA FOR CRAIGSLIST

Be seated on an old futon you no longer want.
Find your centering place . . .
Notice a lumpy, wobbly sensation in your
centering place . . .
When you feel completely uncentered,
visualize rising from the futon and figuring
out how to sell it on Craigslist.

After a count of one second, form an image
of your first reply:
Is the futon still available?
Feel yourself flooded with positivity.
And, slowly, release your positivity . . .
Because you are never going to hear
from this person again.

Now, reshape that first reply into a new reply,
brought forth by a new seeker.
Sense that this seeker seeks answers . . .
He seeks to learn the origin of the futon . . .
And if the futon comes with a certificate of
bedbug inspection . . .
And if you can e-mail more photos from under-
neath the futon.

Observe your resentment rising to the surface, and
imagine crawling under your futon with a camera.
Know that there is no rush to crawl back out . . .
Because you are never going to hear from this
person again.

Now, see yourself rushing home on your lunch
hour because that is when a new futon-seeker
wishes to inspect your futon.
As you move through space, try to paint
a mental portrait of this seeker.
You can't, right?
That is because you are about to get stood up . . .
And you are never going to hear from
this person again.

For the next few moments of our meditation,
simply be present with your Craigslist contempt.
Feel it expanding from within, forming a
phantasmagoria of future futon-seekers:
A seeker who wishes to barter ukulele lessons
in exchange for the futon . . .
A seeker who makes a firm offer of a five-dollar
gift card to Taco Bell . . .
A seeker who wants you to drive it to his house
because he doesn't have a car.

Drape yourself in desperation, and visualize
disassembling your futon . . .
See yourself straining to cram it into your car.
Whenever you are overcome with a hernia
sensation, give yourself permission to toss
your futon to the curb.
See yourself taping a sign on it . . .
A sign that says, "Free."

As your stress disappears along with your futon,
chant Modern Mantra #26 . . .

"I DISPENSE WITH ALL MATERIAL POSSESSIONS I WAS PLANNING TO SELL ON CRAIGSLIST."

I breathe
through the
body odor
of others.

MANTRA FOR THE GENIUS BAR

In the Zen state of nothingness spins a
multicolored wheel of motion.
Concentrate on that wheel as it whirls in the
upper right corner of your frozen MacBook.
With each concentric revolution, feel a scream
forming deep within your throat chakra.

Now, neutralize negativity and flow to a white
expanse flooded with light.
Your arrival to the place is not happenstance.
You are here because the first appointment they
had online was a week from Thursday, so you
figured you'd try a walk-in.

As you are met by a heavily hair-gelled
greeter clutching an iPad, bring awareness to
their words . . .
How's your day going so far?!!
What do you imagine your Authentic Self
would say?
Perhaps your Authentic Self would say, *"It's a
sh*tshow actually, because the f*cking circle on
this piece of sh*t won't stop spinning."*

Slowly, shift back to your Inauthentic Self . . .
Express gratitude for the privilege of waiting
forty-five minutes to see a Genius.

We devote the next forty-five minutes of our
meditation to killing time by shopping for over-
priced wireless speakers we don't need.

Whenever you sense that forty-five minutes have
passed, cultivate happiness.
Now, add another forty-five minutes.
Now, bring your new wireless speakers and your
frozen MacBook to the Genius who is ready to
receive you at the bar.
Picture yourself perched high atop a stool,
secure in the hands of your Genius.

Whenever you sense that yet another
45 minutes have passed, let your mind
wonder if your Genius is really such a genius . . .
As the spinning circle continues to spin and
spin and spin.
Notice your brain spinning along with
the circle . . .
And hear your Genius's voice distorting into
an evil genius's voice:

Corrupted RAM
Insufficient CPU
Logic Board Failure

We complete our Genius Bar journey by bringing
awareness to the fact that our parking meter has
just expired.
And so has our AppleCare warranty.
Today, we open our heart and our wallet to
Modern Mantra #27 . . .

"EVERY PAINFUL JOURNEY TO THE GENIUS BAR BRINGS A HEALING JOURNEY TO THE REAL BAR."

I release
planking.

MANTRA FOR A STAFF MEETING

Conjure your spirit colleagues and travel
to a translucent conference room.
Try not to question the agenda of your meeting.
Simply believe that it may or may not
reveal itself to you . . .
When . . .
And if . . .
It ever ends.

At the head of the table, manifest your spirit
colleague with narcissistic personality disorder.
He is seated at his own imaginary throne . . .
And he is giving a PowerPoint on the many ways
he has saved the company from bankruptcy.
As he pontificates, try to shape-shift him into an
industrial-strength vacuum cleaner . . .
And visualize him sucking all the air out of
the room.

The next spirit colleague we'll hear from in
our meeting meditation takes us on a winding
journey of off-topic tangents.

Form a picture of her bouncing like a pinball
from third-quarter profit strategy to ink
cartridge recycling policy to getting a lock
for the thermostat because someone keeps
making it too cold.
Feel yourself tuning in and out . . .
In and out . . .
While one million e-mails pile up in your inbox.

Whenever you have lost track of the space-
time continuum, imagine your spirit supervisor
forming committees . . .
And putting you in charge of them.
Slowly, feel yourself leaving your physical body.
Free your spirit self to get up from its
ergonomically unsound chair . . .
And to hurl itself headfirst through the glass wall
to the restroom on the other side.

But first, chant Modern Mantra #28 . . .

"THE LONGER THE MEETING, THE STRONGER THE ME."

I am nourished
by scrubbing
barcode stickers
off my produce.

MANTRA FOR
A LITTLE LEAGUE GAME

Power down and behold the wonder of
a child playing ball.
Listen for the magical *swoosh* of his bat
swinging through the warm spring air . . .
And his dad telling the ump to go fuck himself
for calling that swing a strike.

Notice the dad pacing behind the batting
cage like a lion . . .
And taking his child aside to publicly
shame him.
Feel yourself mentally willing the dad into
twenty-four-hour observation by a panel
of licensed professionals.
Attain closure with an image of him getting
ejected for the fourth time this season.

Now, turn your gaze to the colorful cult of
Little League parents in the bleachers.

Be mindful of avoiding eye contact with
each one:
The hopped-up parents who whistle and
whoop and holler . . .
The Major League scout parents who share
scathing commentary on every player except
their own . . .
The sideline coach parents who shout random
and contradictory commands.

Look within and block out the noise.
Feel yourself lifting the index fingers in a slow,
upward motion . . .
And inserting them into your ear chakras.
Hold this position for a count of nine innings.

Whenever you feel centered, remove your
fingers and cheer Modern Mantra #29 . . .

"BE THE CHANGE YOU WISH TO SEE AT THE LITTLE LEAGUE GAME."

A journey of
a thousand miles
begins with
a single step
in dog poop.

MANTRA FOR DIGITALLY DISTURBING THE PEACE

Send yourself on a silent retreat to Costco.
See yourself standing in solitude before a
majestic mountain of paper towels.
Gradually, sense your quietude terminated
by a shopper who is talking to herself.
As she draws nearer, become aware that
she is actually talking to her husband with a
Bluetooth earpiece.
She knows he has been cheating on her . . .
Because she hired a private eye to hack into
his texts.

Now, notice her swerving towards you with
her shopping cart while telling him she
wants a divorce.
If you are tempted to strongly suggest that
she ends her marriage in another aisle,
find the fortitude to hold your tongue.
Begin by releasing the tongue in a relaxed,
dangling manner.
Now, elevate your hand such that it gently
clasps the tongue.
Hold your tongue for a count of ten, and vali-
date your mastery of the mind-body connection.

We continue our silent retreat in a
comfortable train.
Perhaps you are seated in a designated
"quiet car" for a long-distance sojourn . . .
Or perhaps you're unwinding on your
daily commute.

Bring your focus to the violent screams
from a nearby seat.
Listen for the sounds of strong language . . .
And scary background music.
Form a vision of an individual who is watching
The Predator without headphones.
To maintain your serenity at this juncture of
your silent retreat, circle back to the mind-
body connection.
Begin by focusing on your lip . . .
And then, focus on your teeth . . .
Finally, focus on using your teeth
to bite your lip.
Bite your lip for a count of ten.

Our silent retreat culminates with the practice
of self-nourishment.
Envision nourishing the self at a restaurant
because the self is too tired to cook.
Tap into the charming ambience . . .
The sumptuous cuisine . . .
The person Facetiming at the next table . . .

If you feel your silent retreat coming
dangerously close to a confrontational
conclusion, shift the focus one final time to
the mind-body connection.
Keep your body planted firmly at your
own table . . .
But in your mind, recite Modern Mantra #30 . . .

"I AM IMPERVIOUS TO THE PUBLIC USE OF PERSONAL DEVICES."

I dance to
the rhythm
of the all-night
car alarm.

MANTRA FOR JURY DUTY

Today's visualization starts with a pre-visualization
in which you try to get out of today's visualization.
Pre-visualize yourself telling a judicial clerk
that you are scheduled for immediate surgery . . .
And you are the sole caretaker of newborn
triplets . . .
And you are blatantly biased.
With each pre-visualization, release the burden
of Living Your Truth.

Discover the strategy of *Stretching* Your Truth . . .
Embellishing Your Truth . . .
And *Bending* Your Truth into a flexible,
malleable excuse to free you from the shackles
of civic responsibility.

Now, accept that you are powerless over your
pre-visualization, and begin your mandatory
journey of jury duty.
Sequester yourself in a courtroom devoid
of all joy.
Envision a joyless judge, joined in joylessness by
joyless attorneys . . .
A joyless plaintiff and a joyless defendant . . .
And a panel of impartial and joyless jurors you're
stuck with for the next several hours or days.
Or weeks.

Gradually, bring awareness to a sensation of
hypoglycemia.
Pause to ponder if the judge will ever let
you eat lunch.

If you catch yourself craving contact
with the outside world,
recall that your cell phone was seized by
a security guard the second you walked in.

As you return your focus to the courtroom,
feel yourself trying to understand what the
hell they are talking about.
Voir dire . . .
Nolo contendere . . .
Motion in limine . . .

With closing arguments, we connect
with our pain.
It is coming from our buttocks chakra.
Feel the buttocks chakra seated on the hard
wooden bench of a jury box.
Feel as though the buttocks chakra is seated
on a tree stump . . .
Or a cinder block.

Slowly, unleash the buttocks chakra and join
your fellow jurors in a deliberation room.
As you deliberate . . .
And deliberate . . .
And deliberate . . .
Form an image of your life passing you by.
And, now, restore positivity by pleading
Modern Mantra #31 . . .

"BEING SELECTED FOR JURY DUTY VALIDATES ME."

I can
break the
toxic cycle of
posting food
photos.

MANTRA FOR A HOUSEGUEST

Close your eyes and open your home.
Feel your heart swell with loving kindness as
you welcome a cherished houseguest.
Now, imagine it's 48 hours later.

Tap into the tactile sensation of removing wet
houseguest towels from a bathroom floor . . .
Connect with the act of plunging a toilet clogged
with foreign houseguest matter . . .
See yourself extracting a clump of houseguest
hair from a shower drain.

Slowly, shift your attention to the remote control.
Try not to question what your houseguest
pressed to make it not work anymore.
Rather, try to observe yourself darting about
your kitchen on a frantic weekday morning.
Imagine your houseguest sitting around in blissful
serenity as you make a breakfast that conforms
to the many restrictions of their Whole30 diet.

Now, hear your houseguest asking for your
wireless password while you wash their dishes . . .
And reading you an article from their newsfeed
while you're on the phone.
Sense your guest quietly judging your morning
mindfulness practice of fighting with each
member of your family.

And let go into a swirling shame spiral.

We close our meditation by exterminating
our houseguest.
Using guided imagery, reimagine your
houseguest as a house pest.
Begin by visualizing your guest with
insect antennas on their head.
Gradually, add a pair of buzzing wings to your
houseguest's shoulders . . .
Or a hard, crunchy shell to their back.
And now, empower yourself to swat your
houseguest with a fly swatter . . .
Or spray your houseguest with Raid . . .
Or check your houseguest out of your house
and into a roach motel.

When you are satisfied that your dwelling
is no longer infested by your houseguest,
open your eyes and feel the loving kindness
return to your heart.

We restore harmony to the home with Modern
Mantra #32 . . .

"I WILL LIVE EACH DAY LIKE IT IS MY HOUSEGUEST'S LAST."

My pizza
will arrive
whenever it
is meant
to arrive.

MANTRA FOR A NEW PET

Relax on a favorite couch or armchair that has been torn to shreds.
Inhale, and envision an adorable kitten with big eyes and chubby paws.
Exhale, and envision a murdered mouse left at your door like a gift.

Continue this rhythmic, yin-yang breathing pattern.
Now, let your Ch'i flow effortlessly from feline to canine.
Inhale the yin of petting a puppy's furry little tummy . . .
Exhale the yang of finding your shoes gnawed and mangled.
Inhale the yin of being greeted by a wagging tail and wet kisses . . .
Exhale the yang of incontinence.

With each yin-yang breath, surrender the self and connect to the petself.
Connect to the catself . . .
Connect to the dogself . . .
Connect to the self who really should have gotten something easier in retrospect, like a hamster, or a fish.

Breathe in the pet yin, breathe out the pet yang . . .
Breathe in the yin of cuddling with a kitty before bed.
Breathe out the yang of an assailant jumping on your face while you sleep.
Inhale the yin of giving a puppy a treat.
Exhale the yang of a scavenger eating tissues and chicken bones from your garbage can.
And then throwing up.
And then eating the throw-up.

Inhale the hair on your clothes . . .
The hair on your furniture . . .
The hairball on your floor . . .
And exhale an explosive series of sneezes.

We emerge from our pet meditation with a revived sense of balance.
The yin of nurturing a loyal companion . . .
The yang of wanting to return it to the ASPCA before becoming a danger to yourself and others.
Today, we find solace in Modern Mantra #33 . . .

"I CELEBRATE MY PET'S IMPERFECTIONS."

I am
blessed by
the aggressive
activist who
rings my bell at
dinnertime.

MANTRA FOR A CROWDED BEACH

Envision strolling along the shore on a lovely summer's day.

As you stroll, consider how each unique grain of sand is already occupied by someone else.

Slowly, form an image of a patch of sand that is barely big enough for your blanket.

Express gratitude for the sacred space you have found.

Now, envision a large, loud family heading towards your sacred space with an all-terrain shopping cart loaded with beach supplies.

When they intrude into your field of vision, inhale a deep, toxic breath of the banana-scented sunscreen they are spraying into the wind.

Close your eyes and deny their existence.

Notice the soaring seagulls.

Notice how they flock in a scary way at the Doritos the kids are tossing up to them.

Envision a shower of Dorito crumbs gently falling from the heavens and onto your head . . .

Along with the cool, wet droplets of seagull poop.

Next, feel your body tensing up as they shake the sand off their towels and onto you.

Observe the inflatable water toys they stack beside you . . .

And the protective wind tent they pitch right next to you . . .

And the cheap beach umbrella that will soon fly into you.

As you watch the children sprinting back and forth over your blanket with dripping pails of ocean water. . . make time for a moment of mindfulness.

Out of a kajillion souls crammed onto this beach, they have chosen *you*—

not simply to sit next to, but to sit *with*.

We complete our seashore meditation with a domestic quarrel.

Focus on the sound of the parents yelling at each other after finishing their final margaritas.

If you notice a drastic decline in your state of serenity, simply channel your spirit animal.

Perhaps your spirit animal is a swarm of bees that scares them away . . .

Or perhaps your spirit animal is a Doberman pinscher that chases them into the ocean.

Whenever you have finished channeling your spirit animal, return to your practice of nonviolence and chant Modern Mantra #34 . . .

"I AM A SERENE STARFISH ON A CONTAMINATED COAST."

I release
myself from
rinsing
the recycling.

MANTRA FOR ECONOMY CLASS

Find your bliss in a supple leather lounger with limitless leg room.
Breathe in the healing properties of pre-flight hors d'oeuvres.
Hear the joyful pop of a champagne cork.
Welcome a smiling flight attendant who assists with your remote-control footrest.

As you drift off to the magical places within you, awaken abruptly to the swish of a black curtain closing.
Feel the curtain form an impenetrable barrier between you and your foolish first class fantasy . . .
And return to your middle seat by the bathroom.
Notice your knees, pressed against the seat in front of you . . .
Your arms, pressed against the passengers on both sides of you . . .
Your elbows, engaged in an unspoken, high-stakes battle to get the arm rest before they do.

Whenever you are ready, encounter the passenger in the window seat to your right.
She is reading a large, unwieldy newspaper . . .
Flipping each crinkly page into your face.
Imagine her moving the window shade up and down, up and down . . .
So you can never quite see the crappy movie you're trying to watch.
See yourself standing up awkwardly so she can go to the bathroom repeatedly.

Up and down, up and down . . .

Now, shift focus to your snoring seatmate on the aisle.
Feel his head resting gently on your shoulder . . .
And his mouth forming a shimmering droplet of drool.
He is in a deep meditative state . . .
Thanks to four sample-size bottles of Jim Beam adorning his tray table.
Unleash the turbulence brewing inside you.
Connect with your primal urge to shake him violently and tell him you're not a mattress.
And now, release your rage and choose forgiveness.
Because, if you wake him up, he'll talk until the plane lands.

We begin our final descent by manifesting meal service and the beverage of your choice.
Feel nourished by your packet of stale mini-pretzels . . .
And blessed by your cup of burned airplane coffee.
Pause to remember those less fortunate than yourself . . .
Such as the screaming baby with motion sickness behind you.

With your seatback and tray table in their full, upright position, spend the remainder of your voyage chanting Modern Mantra #35 . . .

"I SOAR ABOVE THE INDIGNITIES OF AIR TRAVEL."

I am
soothed
by the song
of the
leaf blowers.

MANTRA FOR A MUSEUM

Retreat to a sanctuary of art, and get in touch with your feelings.
Begin with your feelings of foot pain.
Contemplate your throbbing heels as you stand before a masterpiece.
Slowly, shift the focus to your tiptoes . . .
Feel yourself activating the tiptoes so you can see over a German tour group that is obstructing the masterpiece.
Now, take a deep, yawning breath . . .
And affirm your feeling that there are plenty of other paintings where that one came from.

Next, imagine shuffling into an adjoining gallery filled with ancient earthenware.
The artistry takes your breath away—as though you could black out at any moment because there is no natural air or light.

As you limp to the next exhibit, feel your lethargy transform to animosity.
Direct that animosity toward a pretentious MFA student who looks like Beck,
and who is critiquing the artist's representation of collective objecthood.

Pause here to work on your yawning breathwork.
Visualize a room of Renaissance tapestries that all look the same.

And now, circle back to your aching ankles, by placing yourself in front of some sort of religious mural or whatever it is from some period of history.

We complete our museum meditation by manifesting a rare, cushioned bench.
Give yourself permission to sit on the bench.
As you sit, pretend to ponder the completely blue painting in front of the bench.
Feel your feet begin their healing process . . .
Feel your eyes begin to glaze over . . .
Feel your lids begin to descend.

Finally, from the darkness, see the light . . .
A glowing scarlet light, shining above an open door . . .
A masterpiece of light entitled, *EXIT.*
Walk toward the light, chanting Modern Mantra #36 . . .

"I WILL NOT FALL ASLEEP AT THE MUSEUM."

I have the
grit to stick
my hand down
the garbage
disposal and
get the spoon.

MANTRA FOR A STADIUM SHOW

Transcend the silence and imagine hearing a live performance of your favorite band.
Now, imagine seeing this performance on a jumbotron, because a fellow fan is blocking your view of the stage.
Become aware that he is doing a visualization exercise of his own.
He is visualizing that *he* is in the band.
He is the lead guitarist . . .
And the lead vocalist . . .
And, of course, the lead drummer.

With intention, build a mental barbed wire fence between you and your fellow fan.
Acknowledge your fence's flawed construction when he begins to dance.
See him moving and grooving . . .
Feel him moving and grooving, as he rhythmically smacks you with his air guitar.

With each recurring droplet of beer he spills on you, sense yourself entering a deep state of moistness.

Honor the belligerence building inside you . . .
Notice yourself radiating regret that you spent a hundred bucks for this show on StubHub.

Slowly, form an image of a female fan joining him.
On her feet are the Louboutin heels she will use to step on your toes . . .
In her hands is an iPad she will use to film the show for her Facebook.
Just close your eyes and vibe with the music.
What do you hear?
The two of them screaming the lyrics in your ears?

Feel the tension slowly building in your shoulders . . .
Concentrate on hunching them higher and higher . . .
And now, release.
We endure our arena experience by reciting Modern Mantra #37 . . .

"I DETACH FROM THE DOUCHEBAG AT THE CONCERT."

The nonstop barking dog brings me closer to nature.

MANTRA FOR A TO-DO LIST

Concentrate on your breathing technique
for a count of ten.
When you've reached a count of one,
become aware of a million other things you
should be doing besides concentrating on
your breathing technique.
With each breath, concentrate on each thing.

Inhale . . . *Drop off dry cleaning.*
Exhale . . . *Fill out IRS form 1040A/Schedule D.*
Inhale . . . *Get half-and-half.*
Exhale . . .*Organize 10 years of photos stored
randomly on phone.*

When the rhythm of your breath reveals that you
are hyperventilating, reach deep within.
Reach deep within your pocket . . .
Or perhaps within your purse . . .
Or reach for some complicated app that's
supposed help you stay organized.
For deep within, lies the seed of a to-do list.

Slowly, let your to-do-list take the shape
of a young sapling.
Just as a sapling grows and expands, see your
to-do list growing and expanding . . .
Until it transmogrifies into a towering,
menacing to-do *tree*.

Visualize the long, knotted limbs of errands . . .
The gnarled, thorny vines of obligations . . .
The rotted, fungus-ridden branches of
responsibilities.

Now, bring your conscious attention to a bright,
sunny Saturday.
You are trapped in your hulking to-do tree.
Slowly, manifest a magical, healing ax.
Give yourself permission to hack away at your
to-do tree like a lunatic.
Chopping off the errands . . .
Slashing the obligations . . .
Bludgeoning the responsibilities . . .

We restore serenity with the soothing sound
of a chainsaw.
Unleash your inner power tool until reaching
a sublime state of deforestation.
And now, imagine trucking your to-do tree off
to the mill . . .
And having it pulped into a clean, pure piece
of paper . . .
Which you will inevitably use to write a new
list of things to do.

Today, we put Modern Mantra #38 at the
top of our to-chant list . . .

"I AM GUIDED THROUGH THE DARKNESS BY THE LIGHT OF MY TO-DO LIST."

Spending all day in the doctor's waiting room inspires me to contemplate the passage of time.

MANTRA FOR THE POST OFFICE

Drift back in time to an ancient sanctum
awash in flickering, fluorescent light.
Feel the weight of the unstamped cardboard
box you are clutching.
Notice the calming neurotransmitter of
dopamine depleting from each pore of
your person.

As you take your place in a labyrinthine line,
tune in to a chorus of beleaguered customers
who wish to connect with you:
An elderly neighbor who shares unsolicited
frustrations with Flat Rate, Variable Rate,
Priority Mail, and Priority Mail Express . . .
A soccer mom who feels compelled to complain
about the J. Crew return package she is not
allowed to drop off without seeing a clerk, even
though it is already prepaid . . .
And the reason she is returning it because she
ordered okra and they sent peony.

With each human connection, sense yourself
growing more misanthropic.
Now, set forth to neutralize the negativity.
Picture placing your box on the floor . . .
And searching for your phone . . .

And spending the rest of your time on an
imaginary call to a pretend friend.

When you finally reach the front of the line,
summon the strength to give your box to
the clerk.
Take a moment to ponder if you've ever
been ignored so aggressively by another
human being.
Remember, life is not a rush . . .
At least as far as the post office is concerned.
Just be present.
And just keep being present until the clerk
acknowledges your existence . . .
And refuses to sell you stamps until you tape
your box better.

See yourself selecting a six-dollar roll of
packing tape at the self-service kiosk near
the entrance.
When you have taped the box to the best of
your abilities, visualize bringing it back to the
evil clerk.
And finally, visualize the clerk telling you to
resume your place at the back of the line.
Bitterly, we chant Modern Mantra #39 . . .

"I WILL BE MY BEST SELF, EVEN AT THE POST OFFICE."

The
meaning of
rebuffering will
soon be
revealed
to me.

MANTRA FOR PARKING

Sit upright and go to your happy place.
When you get to your happy place, notice there is nowhere to park.
Continue noticing this for a count of ten blocks.
With each block, feel yourself stretching the boundaries of your happy place . . .
And driving closer and closer to your unhappy place.

Now, bring intention to a person who is sitting in his parked car and talking on his phone.
Visualize pulling up next to him to demonstrate that you desire his spot.
Try not to cloud this moment with expectations that he is ever going to leave.
Simply idle indefinitely.

While you idle, you may catch yourself becoming distracted by an impulse to force open his door, grab his phone, and fling it under a moving bus.
If you experience this sensation, harness the power of mindfulness to will yourself back to your vehicle so you don't get charged with assault.

Gradually, form an image of an empty space.
Embrace the empty space . . .
Parallel park in the empty space . . .
And pull out of the empty space when you notice a cryptic street sign in front of it that says, "No parking any time. 3 hour limit."

Whenever you are ready, admit defeat.
Let go into a steep, spiraling parking structure that costs twenty-five dollars an hour.
With each spiraling ramp you ascend, imagine you are climbing the mystical Himalayas.
Your car, spiraling into the stratosphere . . .
Your rage, spiraling out of control . . .

When you've ascended to the sacred empty space at the peak of the parking structure, express gratitude.
And when a black Escalade careens around the corner and steals the sacred space, express Modern Mantra #40 . . .

"I WILL PICK MY PARKING BATTLES."

I
radiate the
positivity of a
Trader Joe's
employee.

PHOTO CREDITS

Photographs copyright © GettyImages

ACKNOWLEDGMENTS

I'm very #grateful to everyone at Running Press: Jennifer Kasius, Amanda Richmond, Kristin Kiser, Jessica Schmidt, Seta Zink, and Cassie Drumm. I'm also #blessed by those at WME: Jamie Carr, Jay Mandel, and Jennifer Rudolph Walsh.

And don't even get me started about Megan Tingley, Leo Zevin, Josie Zevin, Richard Zevin, Dena Schumacher, Andrea Loigman, Sam Woodruff, Jennifer Melendez, Lisa Chase, Jessica Katzman, Judy Goldschmidt, Keith Summa, Diana Marszalek, Paul Marszalek, Doug Gochman, Adam Lichtenstein, Stephanie Crawford, The Larchmont Public Library, The Mamaroneck Public Library, Elizabeth Sullivan, Tim Rozmus, and Laura Flavin.